Water under Snow

Water under Snow

POEMS

Ralph Stevens

RESOURCE *Publications* • Eugene, Oregon

WATER UNDER SNOW
Poems

Copyright © 2021 Ralph Stevens. All rights reserved. Except for brief quotations in critical publications or reviews, no part of this book may be reproduced in any manner without prior written permission from the publisher. Write: Permissions, Wipf and Stock Publishers, 199 W. 8th Ave., Suite 3, Eugene, OR 97401.

Resource Publications
An Imprint of Wipf and Stock Publishers
199 W. 8th Ave., Suite 3
Eugene, OR 97401

www.wipfandstock.com

PAPERBACK ISBN: 978-1-6667-3084-5
HARDCOVER ISBN: 978-1-6667-2283-3
EBOOK ISBN: 978-1-6667-2284-0

.   DECEMBER 1, 2021 2:32 PM

Drawings by Rebecca Powell

Cover photograph by Sally Rowan

*To the town of Islesford, Maine,
its inhabitants, wild and domestic.*

The world is still here, and there are aspects of human life that are not purely destructive, and there is a need to pay attention to the things around us while they are still around us.

W.S. MERWIN

Contents

Prelude: Chaos Theory | 1

I

Whatever the Dawn | 5
Walking the Main Street of Our Town | 6
In the Mountains | 7
A Grove of Birches | 8
The Photographer | 9
The River | 10
Reversing Falls | 11
The Commonplace World | 12
The Arctic | 13
The Bull Moose | 14
The Loons of North Pond | 15
The Fox | 16
Devices and Desires | 17
A Meditation in Rain | 18
Nocturne | 19

II

The Rain this April Morning | 23
Traveling a Country Road | 24
Waiting for the First Snow | 25
Memento Mori | 26
Bedroom Slipper | 27
Dinosaur Mobile | 28
The Dignity of Old Houses | 29
How Is It That a Ruin | 30
House of Stone | 31
Taj Mahal | 32

III

Magnetic Distance | 35
Eyes on the Song | 36
Death Cleaning | 37
Galesburg, Illinois | 39
The Rain in Movies | 40
Triggering Town | 41
Forgotten until Summer | 42
Sea Chest | 43
This New Year's Morning | 44
All in Good Time | 45
At a Window | 46

IV

Advent 2, 2020: The Trees Wait | 49

Wild Horses | 50

"And Is This All I Get?" | 51

The Window | 52

Water under Snow | 54

Heavy with Last Night's Rain | 55

Three Bicycles | 57

If Even the Stones | 58

Graceland | 59

World Enough and Time | 60

Envoi: Sea Smoke | 61

Acknowledgements and Thanks | 63

Prelude: Chaos Theory

*A butterfly flaps aimlessly
across a field in China
and a dust storm gathers
over the Great Plains.*

It's not what anyone would call
music, the cries of crows and gulls,
frantic and random,
over the beach at sunrise
and I'm no translator, but
there might be a language,
syntax of wings, black and white,
pulling the littoral into words
about what lies on and under
rocks and waves,
a cloud of confabulation
that for all I know
speaks of things succulent and salty,
while in a distant sanctuary organ music
rises in response to these hymns,
these hungry cries.

I

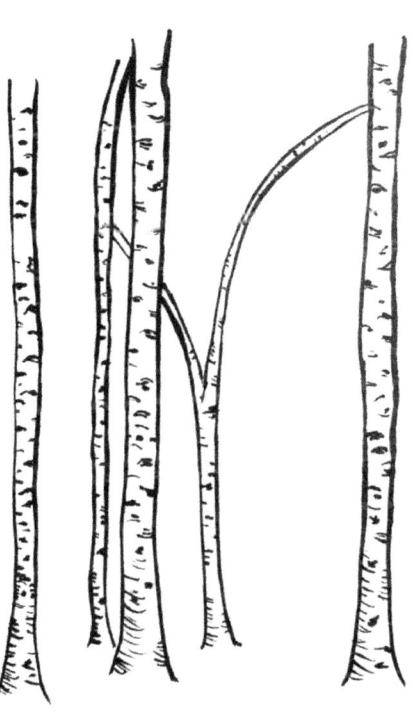

Whatever the Dawn

Walking from sleep to waking
always there are feet
to trip over, hands
dragging me back, voices
whispering it is better
to just lie here and forget
the world outside your small
country of sheet and mattress.
But why can't that world speak up,
drown out the whispers?
Where is the clean, sweet voice
of sunrise, dew on the grass,
the chorus of blackbird or
garden warbler? But the world
for all its sweetness never insists
and if the morphine of the cool
sheets grows from a whisper
to a cry for more sleep perhaps I
should listen with a larger heart,
sort out the words that speak,
however softly,
of hope in the world's charity,
whatever the dawn,
red sky or blue.

Walking the Main Street of Our Town

for morning coffee with a friend
I ask the pavement, trees, the houses
for whatever song they might sing, or
that I might sing to them. It may be
a foolish faith, that we could know
the same music, I and these
quiet creatures, but I listen anyway,
to the mushrooms that appeared
after last night's rain,
moss collecting on a neighbor's roof,
that lawn of snow drops
outside the chapel, flags
waving at the graves of veterans.
And the far-off voice
of hidden water for the desert flower,
of rivers clapping their hands,
the song of emptiness,
of silence between the stars.

In the Mountains

For Andy

And there are times when
I'd rather be in some dark hollow
as in Appalachia, a place where
there is no equatorial sunshine.
About dark places, I've learned
there may not be a way out.
No fumbling with the lock,
willing the door open.
So instead I take the way in,
find these mountain walls
promise a kind of freedom.
I follow the sound
of a Tennessee run
to where it spills over a cliff.
The water sparkles white
on black stone and
sings about a home
locked in mountain shadows.

A Grove of Birches

For Sally

She leaves the house,
me with a stack of books,
and the monotonous drip of rain.
Heading south she
sees a grove of birches
and pulls off the road,
reaches for her phone
in the evening light.
She says she is surrounded by trees,
their slender bodies,
delicate skin. She's not
in any hurry and
how often does she
get to stand by herself
in a birch grove?
The sky has cleared;
she's going to stop a while,
and wait for the moon.
"It will be full tonight,"
she says,
"and will light up the trees."

The Photographer

Again, for Sally

The only imperative that nature utters is, "Look. Listen. Attend."
—C.S. LEWIS

She isn't trying to save the world
as she climbs out of the car,
and walks toward the rocks.
Salvation is in looking, so she
pays attention, takes in the
muted shades and shapes of granite,
subtle humps and sharp edges,
gray or beige, backed by the green
of spruce, the interspersed white
of birches, and out there
the curving surf of the blue Atlantic
where horizon frames the whole.
The world's beauty makes no claim
to beauty, asks nothing
of the viewfinder except
her open eyes.
What can she do but
hold her breath in silence
and raise the camera?

The River

I grew up mindful.
"Mind your manners,"
they said. "Mind you don't
walk in that puddle."
And didn't I learn quickly
how to mind my dad
telling me to sit up straight
at dinner, or, "Look at me
when I'm talking to you."
I practiced mindfulness, paid attention
to what I said, although
the river didn't seem to mind
when I showed up.
It made room for my canoe,
didn't tell me to mind the current,
swift and treacherous.
But I minded everything,
the kingfisher chattering from a branch,
sap in the pine bark,
the way swallows could
turn sharp as glass cracking
when they fed on slow-flying things.
I minded the stench of mud flats,
the sword grass that could slice,
kept it all in mind, forest,
marsh, and river, my breathing
and the breath of evening
as I paddled home.

Reversing Falls

How could I have known
what the river would tell me?
But I ran the reversing falls,
kept the canoe upright in
white water and then drifted,
the paddle across my knees
while the river
found its way home.
And there are currents
that carry us away from
self, all self-
knowing and all need
to know. The heron
stalking the shore
saw nothing but his dinner
darting in the shallows,
and the doe with two fawns
left her mind in the dark of trees
to stare in my direction.
I gave up thinking then and sat,
yielding to the river, the forest,
to whatever was rapid
or still.

The Commonplace World

Disguising the brown lawn and fallen leaves,
snow slowly blanks the ordinary.
A tricycle in the yard disappears, toy trucks
abandoned when October arrived,
a lawn mower someone
forgot to put away.
They fade in eerie silence,
the flower pots,
brick walk where they sit,
picnic table and benches,
putting on layers of white
beside the grill of August's
barbecue. By evening
someone standing on the porch
will see no more than the faint
outline of an Adirondack chair,
and will take that image into the house,
recalling the commonplace world,
beneath the uncommon snow.

The Arctic

*Arctic: . . . from Greek **arktikos**, from **arktos** bear, Ursa Major, north . . .*
—MERRIAM-WEBSTER'S DICTIONARY

How is it that the grizzly cub
is born out of the warm tide
of its mother's blood,
the roar of her heart,
into the wilderness?
I was in the room
when my cubs were born
into the shock of a bright
incubating space. In the Arctic
the bear's blind body crawls
from the darkness of the womb to the icy
brilliance of northern constellations,
to the pounding mountains,
salmon-crowded rivers,
to a light with no walls
to hide it.

The Bull Moose

standing in the high school parking lot
might have told the teenagers
lining the windows that
nature is full of the unexpected.
Bored with physics and
foolish with lust we were not
listening to any wildlife
other than our hormones. That moose
should have been knee-deep in a lake
in the north woods, out of sight
of restless adolescents only too happy
with any excuse to leave our desks.
Impatient with the clock's slow hands we
were content with the novelty itself,
deaf to the larger question
about moose navigation skills.
If that bearded, antlered giant
was lost, well so were we,
lost in wonder
at what the world could deliver
to a small New England town.

The Loons of North Pond

For Sydney

She decides this lake
is a kind of pasture.
Loons graze along the shore and
out there where sweet fish
are offered to the beak.
They are not sheep or cows
and the grasses where they nest
would not nourish livestock
but this lake is pastoral
without the ancient tropes
of shepherds and their flocks.
A golden age lies in these waters,
below the surface, and in the circle
of modest cabins, their kayaks and canoes
grounded now while people
stir and dress, make coffee,
lit by sunrise and
the morning's silence.
She stands on the shore
ignoring the world's undertow—
insults of politicians, shootings in malls,
the cries of children,
torn from their families,
then launches her kayak,
picks up a paddle,
and joins the loons.

The Fox

appeared in the snow
while we boys were inside
with nothing more startling
than breakfast cereal.
But there he was,
looking up at the house,
at the window where we stood
looking back, astonished.

When it's time
to just get up and leave,
not slamming the door but
with no other weapon against pain,
time to walk for hours after midnight,
ignoring the few cars that pass
ignoring me, I remember that fox
stopping in the snow
to look up at the house where
my brother and I ate breakfast,
collected our books,
and left for school,
with red on white
burning our eyes.

Devices and Desires

The snow that fell last night
has covered the brown grass,
scars in the road where pot holes
were filled, the roof of the house next door
with its thinning shingles, worn black
by beating rain.
We sit here just looking
at that spotless expanse, as if snow
never shrank away in the sun.
As if our eyes would not grow tired
of pure appearance and might forget
the dented earth beneath.
Is it an intimation of paradise this
delight, waking to the world
immaculate? And what of other
transformations, after the snow
melts and trees and lawns
are green again? Are these
Eden's residuals, an act of mercy
to give us hope?
Or are they only
the devices and desires
of our hearts?

A Meditation in Rain

It drips from the roof,
steady as an engine idling,
a reassurance as of onions frying,
of radiators ticking, warming up
in a cold dawn. It is
the faint sound of deer feeding
on the buds of saplings
in the spring, or the sound
of glaciers calving, ice waking
after endless sleep. And what of
the roar of an avalanche late at night
after the skiers have gone to bed
so tired they cannot hear it?
Perhaps the rumble
of a giant dwarf star
collapsing in a galaxy
a hundred light years away,
on earth no more than the rustle
of the homeless man on his cardboard,
of sparrows finding a house,
the swallow building a nest,
where her young will crack the shell
of their silent world.

Nocturne

The trees are not sleeping well tonight.
Perhaps it was the dark purple of sunset,
the rising of a blood moon.
I sensed a trembling in the heartwood
and went through the house
looking for something to sing to them,
but couldn't find the music.
The crickets are silent now.
Only an owl has any voice
and he doesn't reassure
the branches where he keeps watch.
I leave the house to sit with them,
the restless trees,
to think out the night and
share their uneasiness,
until the dark has lifted.

II

The Rain this April Morning

is mixed with snowflakes,
falling like blossoms, like
the peach blossoms that fell
on the dead and wounded around Shiloh,
as the cries and yells,
the musket fire,
faded in an uncivil war.
But those little flowers
on bodies lying under trees
meant no irony, no more than did
the little congregation who
named their church "Peace" although
a battle would be fought
in their peaceful orchards, the dead
be covered in peach blossoms.
I remember them now,
those dead and dying,
as this April rain
mixes with snow
and falls on the grass
just starting to turn green.

Traveling a Country Road

. . . or to an illegible stone.

—T. S. ELIOT

The tour of this small graveyard
could turn you nostalgic, relishing
the plaintive sentiment, the
syrup of melancholy.
But see how the rain
has ploughed these head stones,
erased once-sharp outlines
of dates and names.
And doesn't it
tickle your morbid fancy
to spell these elements of decay,
of sure dissolution,
not of flesh alone,
but of the stone that marks
then mocks with its own decay
all thought of resurrection?
It pleases you
to imagine marble slabs
falling on the very graves they
are appointed to point out but
you could just forget
such pleasures, run
at the wind and rain, laughing
at storm clouds, laughing
at what they do
to all these graves.

Waiting for the First Snow

I write a necrology
of the things of summer—
bathing suits taken from the line
and put away, the left-over
bags of marshmallows, hot dogs
buried in the basement freezer.
These aren't dead, exactly,
so I move on to July's wasp nest,
the one the caretaker took care of
with a blow torch.
It's completely gone,
as are the cuttings
from the flower beds.
The grass clippings
tossed on the compost pile
are most certainly dead, and
the laughter at the picnic table
has vanished along with summer's
thick air. Thunderstorms are
over for the year, and it's too cold
to walk barefoot on the beach.
But the wasps are still alive somewhere;
the grass and flowers will reappear.
The beach strewn with seaweed blown loose
in a three-day storm will again be
warm enough for walking.
Outdoor laughter can always
be renewed, the grill be lit
for the first cookout.
But for now the things of summer
will be buried in the snow
starting to fall.

Memento Mori

If I were looking for a way
to picture my mortality, it would not
be this snow now general across
the island, falling slowly in great
flakes to shroud the spruce that stretch
from my back yard to the ocean.
And it would not be the disappearance of
sunlight behind the mountains, the
tearing of the sky from primary
blue to black. No,
I would choose this old sweater
that sheds little dots of wool
as I walk around the house, leaving
a pill trail from the laundry room across
the kitchen and up the stairs, a spot
of sweater skin on every other tread.
It keeps me company on the journey
of getting older, getting thinner and less
able to keep out the cold even as it
marks the return track, waypoints
showing where I've been, the steps from
fear to joy, love to loneliness
and back.
But we're not going back.
We're pressing on
and it doesn't matter which of us
gets there first, which skin finally
sloughs off completely, mine or
this sweater's, and after all,
the wool was once the coat of sheep
living on a wild sea island,
knowing little of the end
of their own woolly journeys.

Bedroom Slipper

When I walk into the room, my young dog
greets me with a bedroom slipper,
still warm from someone's foot.
And what's this pile of fluff?
Real fleece, perhaps.
Perhaps for this housebound hunter
a surrogate for the sheep his
wilder kin would have killed
to keep the pack alive. And does my
innocent pup satisfy his killer instinct
with this inanimate prey?
So be it.
I gladly sacrifice it with the thought
that our human thirst for blood
might be so easily slaked.
What could we offer our enemies,
real or imagined, that might substitute
for the dead and dying, what sort of
common bedroom slipper?

Dinosaur Mobile

As if there were no strings attached
the mobile floats above the kitchen table.
Its cardboard dinosaurs,
red yellow purple blue, drift lazily,
indifferent to the dust they wear
in a house where dusting
rarely happens, and where dust
makes a kind of history
of our presence here.
They go back twenty years, those dinosaurs,
to when we hung them over our newborn son,
and watched him watching them,
their slow dance, learning
to focus his new eyes. We could
keep them dust-free, along with all the
windowsills, chair rungs, base boards, tops
of picture frames, but we don't.
The dust records our lives, things past
and dust coated being present
on a dinosaur mobile,
still drifting in the light
currents of air.

The Dignity of Old Houses

won't be seen on the glossy
pages of decorator magazines,
where the eye grows accustomed
to a certain color balance,
the confident staging of the flower arrangement
on just the right end-table, the rich
but modest sofa, Windsor chair
no one will sit in for very long.
And who's to blame the eye
that can't see past some cracks
in the century-old plaster walls, recoils
at water stains, holes in the ceiling?
The roof line of that old Victorian
is sagging now, appealing only to
a few eccentric photographers.
They walk the hardwood floors
worn bare, admire the carved
but wobbly newel post,
the elegance of the claw foot tub
stained with rust.
It isn't easy to see,
the dignity of old houses.
It needs a certain angle,
a careful distance
        in the slanting
                evening light.

How Is It That a Ruin

You think there's something there,
in the old barn, its roof
sagging in the middle, one wall
collapsing inward.
How is it that a ruin
can arouse your curiosity?
You would not stable horses
in such dilapidation, or ask the cows
to spend even one night.
You know the risk you take now
setting your feet on rotting planks,
looking for you know not what.
The past, perhaps? The last year
that tractor rusting in the corner
came to life and chugged off,
filling the air with blue exhaust?
The old things, the harness,
black leather cracking,
pitchfork attached by spiders
to a post, and clumps of hay
scattered everywhere –
these have the dignity of age.
Age has its privileges
and the privilege of collapsing barns
could be this stillness.
They have earned their independence,
no longer need anything except to sit
with broken tools in the gathering dust,
feeling no obligation
to satisfy anyone's curiosity.

House of Stone

They keep time by standing still,
a thousand ages without moving
but looming, the mountains.
They keep watch.
They block the winds that whistle
through the cracks, around the crags
where snows pile up, where
elk and deer find shelter.
Time plays here as it does with trees
in the valley, as it does with
the wolf, coyote, long-eared rabbit,
with the stone house briefly glimpsed
on a Sunday afternoon.
And it takes its time
while the grass withers,
the mountains ease their way
along eons into dust,
a slow vanishing,
entropy's final act.
It ends in nothing,
after a while,
except in what dust remembers,
as it floats where galaxies once floated –
dust as from a house of mountain stone
that stood for a time after the mason
laid his plumb line down.

Taj Mahal

You wouldn't think,
looking at the four turrets,
the central dome a woman's
perfect breast, that this
would be a place of death.
Somewhere in those white
marble walls is the body,
the remains of the body,
the mere dust of the body,
that inspired this beauty.
And who, after all, was inspired?
Did the architect know the one
who would be entombed?
Something informed the eye that saw,
hands that knew a unity of line,
the straight joined to the curve.
What was the connection, those lines,
and the lines of the body
laid to rest in this mansion,
crown of palaces,
scourge of death?

III

Magnetic Distance

There is a magnetic distance between the word 'woman' and the word 'poet.'
—EAVAN BOLAND

Like the distance between wind and the leaves.
Or between the tire and the road.
Between the crow flying and the crow landing
    on a scrap of bread.
The distance between starlings in a murmur,
    attracted but never attaching.
Between the coffee and its blackness.
Between icicle and sunshine.
A distance between my foot and the creaking floor,
    between the fingers and the piano.
A distance between the throat and "Ah!"
Between a star and its planets, but also
    within the atoms of light.
I see magnetic distance between the old man and
    the cane he holds.
He lowers it to the path never knowing
    when he might stumble.
And the distance between us
    that old man and me
        is magnetic.

Eyes on the Song

So I watch her at the piano,
alive to the music, her fingers
no more than feathers on the keys,
her eyes on the song.
And it's my life I hear as I
turn away, to my high school yearbook perhaps,
with its faces of old friends, reminders
of cruising downtown, fresh from study hall,
the unwrinkled faces of girls,
my serial unconsummated loves.
And it's my life I see, whether morning
or nightlife while I walk a gravel path,
study the meaning of breath and stride,
or sit on a bench to look at my phone.
I follow the progress of a
mother with a stroller,
measure the arc a swing makes
with its laughing pilot.
I find it everywhere,
in a seat on the number 22 bus,
a paddle boat on the lake next door,
walking the ruins of a castle in Wales
on some dreamed-of vacation
with my wife of thirty years, or
in that Chopin nocturne,
with the moon,
about to shatter the horizon.

Death Cleaning

I have death cleaned so many times for others I'll be damned if someone else has to death clean after me.

—MARGARETA MAGNUSSON

The first to go is the shoe polish
which we never use these days.
The shoe rack is down to flip flops,
rubber boots when the weather calls for them.
And bedroom slippers,
which double as driving footwear –
we're like the barefoot boys in "Tom Sawyer"
these days.

Then old magazines, which
we must admit we think we'll read,
but never mind.
We got by for years
without that article about hippies
in geodesic domes; and speaking of hippies,
we really don't need
all those tie-dyed tee shirts or even
the books on organic gardening. It was
a nice thought, the raised beds,
fertilized with our kitchen compost.
And yes, we no longer need
the compost bin, having taken
to throwing food scraps out the back door
for the gulls and crows.

The 50's rock'n'roll
on 45's haven't had much play recently.
Roy Orbison and the Everly's are still classic,
but that brown box record player

died before the last beach party,
replaced by – oh yeah, the boom box.
It's in the attic somewhere. Why
did we hang on to it all these years?
Nostalgia? Perhaps nostalgia
should be the first to go in
all this death cleaning.
Toss it. Nostalgia makes it hard.

But we're going to have a go
at the hard stuff.
Like the photo albums. (Are you
kidding?) The cap and gown from my
college graduation? And all those LP's—
your Beatles albums, Joan Baez . . .
Sure, the old papers—
bank statements, medical records, no problem, but
what about the ashes of our dog
put down when arthritis crippled him,
the sword Dad wore at his
Annapolis graduation, his dress blues?
And speaking of dress,
what about your wedding . . . ?

I'd rather die first.

Galesburg, Illinois

Again, for Sydney

It comes from a teacher in the mountains
just as February starts to drag.
She calls it useless information,
about mixed precipitation and student papers.
She writes of her childhood,
of Galesburg, its Victorian homes,
brick streets with steel rails showing,
a mystery to teenage drivers who
complain about the shock rattling surface,
who've never heard of street cars
running under sparking power lines
along the straight and narrow.
Coal trucks rumbled those streets
to the old Victorians, shouted loads
into cellars' black holes, fuel to feed
furnaces that on winter mornings
would blaze and splinter Galesburg cold,
and bring the children shivering from their beds
as kitchens grew warm, and
that's the useless information
for today.

The Rain in Movies

falls in shock cuts
on people soaked,
drenched bare-headed,
hair plastered against scalps.
Sometimes they carry umbrellas
and I look anxiously
to see if such wobbling shelter
can keep them dry.
Or with no umbrella,
rivulets pouring down their cheeks
as they stand there,
oblivious to the elements, talking
about love or war, the friend they
just visited in the cancer ward or
walking from a dark house where
the dead body lies.
Those people caught
in this mortal coil, the deadly
accidents, family feuds,
betrayals, the mad dash
with a message which might save
some bare forked animal –
they might catch their death of cold, so
why don't they
just come in out of the rain?

Triggering Town

After Richard Hugo

He was convinced a town could
trigger a poem, a town
small enough to focus the mind but
big enough for a few
shops, a post office, diner,
places where people gather,
the carpenter on a coffee break,
widow whose loss has not
kept her from dressing smartly
for the outing to collect her mail.
And here's an old man with his walker.
He had a stroke a year or so ago,
endured hours of rehab,
and now shares with all
his dry humor.
A small town with no pretensions,
facing decline of one sort or another,
children growing into college and
into city life, jobs disappearing
into global corporations.
A town always haunted
by streets lined with for-sale signs,
filling slowly with retirees and yet
still with enough life
to trigger a poem.

Forgotten until Summer

are the empty houses of our town,
forgotten until they pack the car
and arrive, parents and children,
to fill the rooms. Caretakers
will turn the water on,
pull the sheets off furniture
where no one sits now on this
January morning. I am
filled with the emptiness of houses,
cupboards where dishes do not feel
a human hand, closets full of
empty shirts and dresses, rooms
full of silence, air cold, unmoving.
It finds me, this emptiness,
I am drawn to it
in sympathy with the houses
defenseless now,
and full of winter.

Sea Chest

You lumbered uninvited alongside
the woman I married
into a house in a port city
where we made a home.
I endured your presence.
What choice did I have?
You were part of her so I
let you in, with your crude butt joints,
primitive carving of a ship,
banner proclaiming that "Commerce
must be protected."

"Sea chest" we call you,
though you aren't the sort of chest
a man would take to sea.
I've come, in our years together,
to see a colonial bedroom,
a Boston wife, alone.
She waits, while she
washes and irons the sheets
she stores in those
ample drawers,
along with wool blankets,
the cotton nightgowns, dresses
of plain gingham she wears
while she feeds the baby, bakes bread,
while she thinks of her husband
whose ship must be protected,
and who lives now in my house,
in your simple carpentry.

This New Year's Morning

opens with the sound
of slow footsteps on the stairs.
My wife appears, her arms
around a basket of laundry.
She heads without looking my way
for the washer in the smallest
room in the house.
I watch the inchworm growth of icicles
along the porch eaves, study
the drift of snow against the stone wall
my neighbor built last year, a year
now gone, or so we say, telling time
goodbye so we can restart our
lives, ending one dance and
stepping into another,
dance that will become
familiar as footsteps
on the stairs at sunrise.

All in Good Time

For Ben and Milo, Christmas, 2018

I went at your request and out of love
into the shop where years ago we bought
Christmas stockings for the family,
stockings we hung from hooks in the woodwork,
knitted with yarn so heavy and aromatic it recalled
the thick woolen backs of sheep
standing in the rain on a green hillside –
into that shop to buy a stocking for your son.
And everything was on sale,
all the bright wool stockings
gone, swept into other shoppers' bags.
I left the store empty-handed
and sat by the harbor on a stone,
one left behind after the last ice age.
The sun was out, the star that
warmed the glacier
that delivered the stones
that now kept me company,
all in good time.

At a Window

For Ann

I sit and watch her
watch two men and a boom truck
setting a pole.
I want words for the look
on her face, or looks, rather,
as subtle shades of interest flow,
a stream of thought and feeling,
sometimes smooth and deep with concentration,
sometimes rippling with delight.
Her eyes are a river,
a current fast or slow,
peaceful as a river moves.
But you have to see it, her
watching the men working,
wondering now and then what
the pole is for.
I cannot give you her watching
or me watching her, cannot
put you at that window.
What am I doing, then, and why?
I have only my watching,
recollected on a tranquil page,
these words of that watching,
no more than notes in a song,
waiting for the singer.

IV

Advent 2, 2020: The Trees Wait

Ahead of me deer gather,
feed on the last of autumn's leaves.
I wish them winter shelter. It's late.
The geese have flown and loons
have exited the lake
for the coast where home
is waves that never freeze, and
herring are in good supply
The earth makes no complaint
while our north woods fold
into orange and red and then
stand bare. It takes
no imagination to imagine
the lake is listening. I know
what the trees are thinking and
if I pay attention I can
hear them relax,
ready and waiting.

Wild Horses

The morning lies about the house
Gray and sodden as bodies of soldiers
Lying in the rain.

Are there words to charm the day
Into something handsome,
Comely as a herd of wild horses?

There's coffee, bacon frying,
Ordinary comforts,
Not a magic spell.

Whatever clears the eye to see
Through this fog
Won't be spells or coffee.

But there are those horses,
Standing in the shelter
Of cottonwoods.

There is the thunder of hooves
Filling the canyon, the flash
Of dark eyes.

They have no regrets,
The wild horses, for them
All days are handsome.

They see the open meadow;
They know
Where the sweet grass lies.

"And Is This All I Get?"

I asked, sitting at the table,
"just these walls?"
They wore the look
of walls I knew as a child,
standing in the crib,
chewing the varnish as
dusk settled into a room where
they had put me to bed too soon.

So I took my coffee to the porch
and there were people on the road,
unannounced and unexpected,
one in a blue golf cart,
another carrying a suitcase, and a boy
on a skateboard.
They were floating toward me
as if held up by the sky
along with all things plain and customary:
gravel on the shoulder,
dandelions on the lawn, and now
the doctor's wife on a bicycle,
her retriever on a leash
trotting beside her.

The Window

After "Danse Russe" by W.C. Williams

What comes to mind this morning
is Dr. Williams' solitary dance.
I spend a lot of time
alone in my room but
I do not dance naked
in front of a mirror
nor did, not even when
I was slim enough,
skin smooth enough
to be a source of admiration.
After all, it can be risky
looking in the mirror at
my naked body. Someone
might look in accidentally
and wonder what
I could possibly see in myself,
hopping about like that.
I'd sooner leave the body,
smooth or wrinkled, naked or
in flannel pajamas,
and turn to the window.
It opens to a view of the lake,
to the dock, a canoe
resting on it, birches
white along the shore.
Dancing in the mirror, I would
miss the family of loons
swimming out from the reeds.
The parents lead the chicks
in what I imagine is
a morning lesson in diving.
The water is mirror flat but

they ignore what it reflects
in favor of what a loon sees
before it disappears
below the surface.

Water under Snow

I've become ... more willing to grow old.

—MARY OLIVER

You might think this day
has no reason to be any different.
There are the same
snowbanks along the road,
patches of ice you thought would be
gone by now, the same gray trees—
not the ones that will bud
green in a month, but the
dried up ones that remind you of kindling
in the kitchen wood box.
And the houses sit where they always
sit, wearing the same white siding,
green trim, same fading shingles.
And here you are,
on another morning walk
trying to shake off the same
old thoughts, asking
is this the way the world ends,
wearing nothing but gray, except
you pick up the sound of water
running under the snow,
a low chuckle like the pink of sunrise,
something that wasn't
there before, and you
are now more willing
to grow old.

Heavy with Last Night's Rain

And so it was
after hours of walking
there in the road:
the apple of despair.
Or was it a chestnut?
I can't remember now
so many years it's been.
I picked it up
thinking I knew despair and
could handle it, but
not by throwing it
into the woods.
A deer might find it, or
a porcupine, a snuffling
hedgehog. For the
wildlife along that road
there was already lurking
the shadow of despair.
The world grew old with all
the illnesses of age so I
went on, holding the orange, or
was it an egg, unbroken,
of despair, knowing it
takes many forms.
Besides, I wasn't ready
to release it into that landscape,
the forest so quiet, the meadow
misted as the rising sun fell
on grass heavy with last night's rain.
I walked then with despair
lying still in my hand
the grapes or
perhaps cherries
growing dry

starting to shrivel
as the village and
my own fields
came into view.

Three Bicycles

I look out the window to an overcast sky.
Three bicycles glide from the gravel road
beside the house, in a place where we wait
a long time for the light.
Is it just a melancholy humor talking?
Or is my life really a dung beetle
feeding on sorrow, a kind of
droppings of the happier moments
that pass like those bicycles?
My own wheels spin, keeping me
balanced while the light gathers
the way the footsteps of the jailer
gather as he approaches the cell where a man
waits for news of his parole.
It will arrive, breaking through this
cloud, the light that follows
people on bicycles,
or shines on the lobsterman
who finds six keepers in one trap,
that breaks over refugees greeted at the door
of a foreign shelter. The light
that warms the room
where a man wakes up to learn
he has another day to live.

If Even the Stones

Luke 19:40

If even the stones
can cry out, then
there must be blood
in a stone, in its past
when it was conceived or
at the birth of stone,
before it turned hard
against wind and rain.

Now a residual cell
deep in the heart of stone
nudges a neighbor and says
"The world is good so
why is it quiet here, where we
pave the streets of the city?
Where did this light
come from and why
does no one shout for joy?
It must be time for us
to have our say."

Graceland

*But I've reason to believe
we all will be received
in Graceland*

—PAUL SIMON

When I've had it
with feeling different,
walking splay-footed and
too easily offended or
offensive, I consider
the Milky Way.
I hear my wife's voice
lift like a Mozart sonata
when she looks at the night sky,
and I understand the grace
she knows, held in chords free
of trouble, telling me that
I'm not tied to earth by
every failed ending, that
I'm under no obligation now.
I'm free to look away,
to look up because
we all will be received
in the heaven she sees,
outlined in that stretch of stars.

World Enough and Time

While we have world enough and time,
let's learn to talk to the crows.
They gather in the trees this evening
as they always do, gossiping.
Perhaps they're talking about me,
who just threw out some scraps.
And what about the trees?
Do we have time
to learn the words they use
to talk about the crow family
living in tree houses?
And then there are the stars.
They must have a language of sorts.
The sun is going down now,
shining on the back
of the stop sign at the corner,
its light flashing as the sign
shakes in the evening breeze.
I do not know the words
stars speak, but I know about fire,
that flames can talk. So I listen
as the earth now turns its back
on the star we call ours.
That ball of fire signals something to us,
a comment about what the world looks like
from up there.

Do we have time
to learn the language of the stars?

Envoi: Sea Smoke

Poems moor unseen like fishing boats
on a day so cold the thin
harbor vapors become sea smoke.
Standing on the dock,
wondering what I'm doing here
in sub-zero weather, I catch the outlines,
shadows of boats riding –
riding nothing but air.
I know the water
is down there in the smoke
holding those boats
the way earth holds the trees
and sends the fire of nitrogen
into their roots. I wait
for a poem to snap its mooring,
float out of the smoke,
blazing.

Acknowledgements and Thanks

THE FOLLOWING POEMS ORIGINALLY APPEARED in *Verse Virtual: An Online Community Journal of Poetry*: "A Meditation in Rain," "Devices and Desires," "Heavy with Last Night's Rain," "How Is It that a Ruin," "Forgotten Until Summer," "Memento Mori," "The Arctic," "The Window," "Three Bicycles."

"Galesburg, Illinois" appeared in a slightly different version in *Verse Virtual* as "The Useless Information for Today."

"The Commonplace World" originally appeared in *The Ellsworth American*, January 9, 2020.

It needn't be said that a wise writer seeks the help of careful readers. I am grateful for the attention to these poems, and for the insightful suggestions, of Tom Bertrand, Andy Kohn, and Elizabeth Phelps.

Encouragement and support come from many quarters. I want especially to thank, in addition to my three readers, the following: Jeanne Kohn, William McKeachie, Ben Stevens, Tom Trzyna, Alan Walowitz; Matthew Wimer and Jonathan Hill at Wipf and Stock for their ready help; and Rebecca Powell, who took time from raising a family, and from her work as an art director at Gordon College, to provide the art for this book; and the friends too numerous to mention whose comments over the years have helped sustain my writing.

Inspiration for a poem comes from a wide range of sources. I want especially to thank Sydney Landon Plum, whose poignant comments on life and poetry over the years have prompted many of the poems in this collection. And to my wife, Sally Rowan, thanks for her expert proofreading, and deep gratitude for her inspiring love of the natural world and for the camera that accompanies her.

A final note: I wish to acknowledge my debt to two fine poems, Thomas Hardy's "During Wind and Rain" and George Herbert's "Church Monuments," for imagery and language used in "Traveling a Country Road."

www.ingramcontent.com/pod-product-compliance
Lightning Source LLC
Chambersburg PA
CBHW071743040426
42446CB00012B/2458